التوبة

REPENTANCE

(TAUBA)

Selection from
Ihya Uloom- Id- Din

IMAM AL- GHAZALI

Qadeem Press

Qadeem Press

Qadeem Press Edition
Breathing Life into Forgotten Pages
www.qadeempress.com

Reprinted by Qadeem Press in 2025

Find our titles on your favourite online bookstore using the keyword 'Qadeem Press'

Contents

Tauba (Repentance)....7

Meaning of Tauba....7

Four Principles of Tauba....7

First Principle - From of Tauba, knowledge, and limit....8

Merits of Tauba....9

God is Agent of Actions....13

Tauba is compulsory....14

Branches of faith....15

Examples of a Sinner and a Virtuous Man....15

Compulsory Tauba's Systematic Descriptions....18

Meaning of Wajeb....20

Condition of Acceptance of Tauba....23

Saying of Sages....25

Tauba from Minor and Major Sins....27

Classes of Sin according to the Nature of Men....27

Firstly- Godly nature....28

Second class of sins....28

Third class of sins....29

Major sins have got three stages....30

Punishment and Reward in the Next World....32

Man will be divided into Four Classes in the Next world....34

Stages of Those Who Will Meet with Destruction....35

Second stage. 36

Different stages of the Fortunate 38

Causes of Disasters on Religious People 39

Persons who get salvation. 42

Rewarded persons. 43

When a Minor Sin turns into a Major Sin? 44

1. The first cause 44

2. The second cause 44

3. Third cause 45

4. The fourth cause 45

5. The fifth cause 46

6. Sixth cause. 46

Conditions of Tauba 48

Determination or firm will. 49

Breach of duties towards the people. 50

Regarding property. 52

Determination in Future 53

Classes of Repentants 55

1. The First Class of Repentants: 55

2. The second class of repentants. 56

3. The third class of repentants: 57

4. Fourth class of repentants: 58

Expiation of Voluntary and Involuntary Sins 58

Different stages of seeking forgiveness. 60

Medicine for Unwillingness to Repent 61

Disease of the soul. 64

There are Four Modes of Giving up Sins. 65

1.The first mode - 65

2. Second mode: 66

3. Third mode: 69

4. Fourth Mode: 71

The second root is patience: 75

Causes of Commission of Sins 76

1.First cause: 76

2. Second cause: 76

3. Third cause: 77

4. Fourth cause: 77

5. Fifth cause: 77

Tauba (Repentance)

Meaning of Tauba

Tauba means repentance for a sin by making a promise not to do the same evil again and to return to God. Repentance is the beginning in the life of a person who intends to walk in the path of religion. It is the root of the fortune of those who are successful, the first step of a disciple, the key to guidance to the straight path, the weapon of purification of those who wish to come close to God, and a dear thing of all Prophets. So, it is no wonder that man will commit sins. Hazrat Adam introduced the rule of repentance, and he repented for the sin he committed in the past. It is necessary for man to return to God penitently after the commission of sins. He who does good deeds is close to God, and he who always does sinful deeds is close to the devil. He who does good deeds after commission of a sin is a real man.

Four Principles of Tauba

Human nature is mixed up of two elements. Every man has got the nature of angel, nature of man and nature of devil. He who does always sinful acts keeps connection with the devil. He who does always good acts keeps connection with angels. Nothing can give salvation to a man except the fire of repentance.

So, repentance or Tauba has got four cardinal principles.

1. The first principle is from of repentance, its limit, and its knowledge. It is the bounden duty of a man to make repentance after sin. If it is sincere, it is accepted.
2. The second principle is to turn away from sins, to know the major and minor sins, to know the duties towards God and to

men, to know means progress and retrogression for virtues and vices and to know the causes of minor sins turning into major sins.

3. The third principle is to know the condition of Tauba, search into past sins, expiation of sins and the classes of those who repent.
4. The fourth principle is to know the causes of making Tauba and the medicines of persons addicted to vices.

First Principle - From of Tauba, knowledge, and limit

Repentance consists of three elements- knowledge condition and action. Knowledge of Tauba is necessary for condition, as condition is necessary for action. God promulgated this rule in the physical and spiritual worlds. Knowledge is necessary for repentance that the harms of sin are very severe. When you will know it with faith and truth, you will then become repentant for losing an object of love. When repentance prevails over the mind, another condition arises in mind which is called will or desire. It has got connection with present, past and future actions. Its connection with the present means that he wills to give up the sin which he has committed. Its connection with the future means that he becomes determined to give up to the last stage of his life the sin for which he is to be separated from his dear ones. Its connection with the past means that he wills to make expiation for not doing an action which he should have done.

So, to know and search for doing good deeds as mentioned above is the first condition. This knowledge means faith and certainty of belief, as the meaning of faith is to know with truth that sin is destructive like poison. The certainty of belief means to believe as sure the immutable truths. The light of this faith is enkindled in the heart when the fire of repentance rises up. As a result, his heart becomes dejected. He becomes then like a person who remains in darkness and then the rays of the sunshine on him or he sees his beloved if the screen is removed from him.

So, knowledge, repentance, and determination have got connection with the giving up of sin in the present and future and repentance of the past sins. If these three elements are united in a person in an orderly manner, it is called Tauba or repentance, but most people confine Tauba within repentance and do not consider the other two elements. The Prophet said: Tauba means repentance. It is such a fire of repentance as burns the heart and even attacks the back- bone. Hazrat Sahal Tastari said: To change bad habits into good habits is Tauba. Solitude, silence and eating lawful things are conditions of perfection of Tauba.

Merits of Tauba

Tauba is Wajeb or compulsory. There are different classes of sojourners of religion. (1) One class are shot-sighted. They cannot cross their blind faith at every step. So, the Quran and Sunnah of the Prophet are necessary for them at every step. (2) Another class of sojourners are fortunate. God expanded their breasts for Islam, and they are upon light from their Lord and cross the impregnable stages of the path with care at the slightest hint. The light of the Quran and faith shines upon their hearts. A slight hint is sufficient for them owing to the brilliance of light. They know that repentance is compulsory in order to gain permanent good fortune and security from permanent ruin. The meaning of Tauba is to give up sins and to determine to do good deeds.

God says: O believers, be repentant to God all together that you may get salvation - 24 31. God says: O believers, repent to God with sincere penitance-66: 8. Sincere penitence means to return to God from sin in order to in our pleasure of God in a condition free from doubt. God says: God loves those who are penitent and pure - 2: 220. The Prophet said: A penitent man is dear to God. He who returns from sin is like one who has got no sin.

The Prophet said: Think that a man went to a vast field with a camel loaded with food and fuel. He slept thereafter leaning his head. When he awoke, he did not find his camel there. Then he began to search for it, running to and fro, and said after getting tired of hunger and sun: I will go to my former place to sleep, such a sleep that it may cause my death. Then he placed his head upon his hands and slept there to meet with death. When he awoke, he found his camel standing before him with food and water. His joy then knew no bounds. God becomes more pleased with the repentance of a believer than his joy. In another narration, the Prophet said: He was beside himself with joy and said in an ecstasy of joy I am your Lord and You are my servant.

Hazrat Hasan Basri said: When God accepted the penitence of Adam, the angels blessed him and Gebriel and Michael came to him and said: O Adam, God accepted your repentance and cooled your eyes. Adam said: O Gebriel, what will be my rank if after acceptance of this repentance some questions are asked? God then revealed to him: O Adam there will come sorrows and difficulties over your followers and repentance will be open to them. Whoever among them will repent, I will accept his repentance as I have accepted yours. Whoever seeks My forgiveness, I will not be miser in accepting his forgiveness as I am near and accept invocations. O

Adam, When I shall resurrect the repentant men, they will smile and enjoy, and their repentance will be accepted.

Tauba is compulsory according to the unanimous opinion of the jurists. It means to have knowledge that sin and disobedience to God are harmful and remove the sinner away from God. This appertains to compulsory faith. Tauba is firm determination to give up sin in the present and future and repentance for past sins. This shows that Tauba is compulsory.

Question. Has man got freedom of action?

Answer. Man has got freedom of action, but it is not opposed to our opinion that everything is the creation of God and man's freedom of will is also the creation of God. When man wishes, his wish has been created for him. For instance, God created hand, sound, and delicious food. He created in mind this Knowledge that the greed will be pacified by this food. He also created the contrary thought whether it would be good or injurious if the greed for food is satisfied and whether this kind of food is agreeable or not. He also created this understanding whether it has got any bar or not. If these causes are united, there comes the will to take that food. As a result of two conflicting thoughts and the greed for food, will comes in and that is called freedom...of will. When all the elements are fulfilled, there comes will. When God creates the will and makes it firm, He allows his sound hand to extend towards food, as the unification of will and strength leads compulsorily to action. These two things, will and strength, are the creations of God.

Out of these creations, one thing is guided to another according to a well-arranged plan created also by God. There is no change of God's plan. He does not move the hand to a well-arranged writing, till He creates strength in it, till He gives it life, and till He creates firm will. He does not raise up firm will till He creates greed in mind. He does not create this greed fully till He creates this knowledge or understanding whether it will conform to nature in the present or future. He does not create this understanding without other causes which make movement of limbs, will and knowledge. So, understanding and desire of mind follow firm will and strength. Will comes before movement of bodily limbs. This rule is prevalent in every action. So, everything is created by God and one thing of his creation depends upon another thing. For instance, will comes after understanding, understanding comes after life, and body comes before life. So, the creation of body is necessary for life but not life for body. Similarly, creation of life is necessary for creation of understanding and not creation of understanding for life. Understanding does not come if there is no life. Understanding has been created to make will, firm and not for creation of will. Will does not come without life and understanding.

When nature is subject to some condition, the condition is created to accept that nature. Then that nature can be acquired from the strength of fate and God-given gift. When nature has got uniformity owing to the cause of condition, so also there is uniformity for occurrence of an event owing to the action of God. Man should necessarily be fit for occurrence of this uniformity. God says: I have created everything according to a measure. With regard to the original fate, there is this verse: My order is not but in a twinkling of an eye. Man is subject to his fate owing to this fact or pre- measurement. He created the strength of movement in the hand of a writer after creation firstly of an attribute named strength, secondly after creation in his mind a firm determination and thirdly after creation owing to this determination in mind understanding and fourthly knowledge of cognition. When these four matters subservient to fate from the unseen world appear in the body of a man, the inhabitants of the world know it. But before it remains hidden in the unseen world. Then the inhabitants of this world say: O man, you have moved, you have thrown arrows, you have written, but proclamation comes from behind the screen: When you have thrown arrows, you have not thrown them. It is God who has thrown them. When you fought, you have not fought. It is God who have fought with them. God will punish them through your hands.

God is Agent of Actions

Then the superficial learned man becomes blind and understands it. From his standpoint, he says that man has got freedom of will. Some say that man has got freedom of will but has got no connection with pre-measurement or destiny. Some adopt the middle course and say that man's action is subject to efforts. If the doors of heaven would have been opened to them and they looked to the spiritual and unseen world, it would have surely been disclosed to them that every opinion is true from one standpoint or the other, but there is defect in it. God knows the open and secret worlds. He does not disclose it except to those prophets with whom He is pleased. He who has entered the limit of His pleasure knows only the things of this world and not of the spiritual world. But a man of spiritual world knows that God is the Creator of everything and there is no master of action except He.

Question. You have said that every opinion is true. Cite an example for clear understanding.

Answer. Know, O dear readers, that a party of blind men went to see an elephant which they had never seen before. When they reached the elephant, they touched it. One blind man touched its feet, another its ear, another its trunk. They at once exclaimed: We have known an elephant. When they went away, other blind men asked: How is an elephant? They all described its different forms. The blind man who touched its feet said that the elephant is like a post. The blind man who touched its trunk said: The elephant is not as the other blind man has described. The elephant is a hard substance and not a post and it is long. One who touched its ear said: By God, the elephant is smooth like a sieve The saying of each is true in some respect or the other, but none could give a full description of an elephant. The difference of many men over a single matter is like this. This gives clue to spiritual knowledge.

Tauba is compulsory.

Tauba is compulsory with its three ingredients, knowledge of sin, repentance for sin and giving up of sin in future. Tauba is compulsory after commission of sin, as a believer can understand that sin is harmful. He who does not give up sin gives up a portion of faith. The following Hadis proves it. When a man commits fornication, he commits when he is not a believer. That fornication is injurious like poison* is not known to him. This is said with regard to the faith which returns to spiritual knowledge. At the time of commission of fornication, he loses faith that fornication is injurious and that it keeps him far away from God, just as when a physician says: It is poison and don't take it. If in spite of this warning, a person takes it, it can be said that he has taken it as he disbelieved it. This does not mean that he does not believe in the existence of the physician or that he has got no knowledge of medicine, but it means that he does not believe that poison is harmful, as he who knows the effect of poison, cannot accept it.

Branches of faith.

There are more than seventy branches of faith. The highest branch is there is no deity but God, and the lowest branch is to remove injurious things from pathways. This truth is found from the following instance. A man is not composed of one thing only but with more than seventy elements. The highest element is soul and life, and the lowest element is removal of undesirable things from the body, such as trimming moustache, manicuring, nails etc. Faith is also like a man. The highest element of it is Tauhid. Faith does not remain if Tauhid goes just as a body does not live if life goes out of it. He who has got only Tauhid is like a man chopped of hands and feet and he is near death. Similarly, if a person has got nothing except basic faith, his tree of faith is about to crumble down if a great tempest attacks it, or it faces the angel of death. Faith of one, if not established upon firm foundation and not expressed in actions does not stand firm at the great tempest or the attack of the angel of death. The condition of his end becomes fearful. The faith which is watered constantly by divine services remains intact at the time of death.

Examples of a Sinner and a Virtuous Man

If a sinner says to a virtuous man: I am a believer as you are a believer, his saying is just like the saying of a creeping plant to a big tree: I am a tree just as you are a tree. The big tree says to the creeping plant:

You will know soon false is your claim. At the time of tempest your root will be uprooted. The tree of Arefin or agnostic has got the fear to be cut off even at their advent of death. He who is a sinner does not fear to live forever in Hell. His condition is like that of a sound man who remains immersed in harmful passions and low desires, as he does not fear death owing to his robust health. He should be said this: A sound man should fear illness and death may come to him if disease attacks him. Similar is the condition of a sinner. He should fear his end and consequent punishment in Hell.

So, he who commits sin having faith is like the eater who eats food injurious to health. Thus, it continues till he meets with sudden death. Similar is the condition of the sinner. When you give up the food in this world mixed with poison as injurious, how much necessary is it for you to give up sins which are injurious in the next world? He who eats poison and becomes repentant disgorges it from his stomach by vomiting it at once. When this is necessary in this temporary world, how much necessary is to give up sins which are detrimental to the immortal soul? To repent for sins during lifetime is necessary because sin like poison will destroy the ever-lasting happiness of the next world. If the next world is destroyed, one shall have to enter burning fire and receive other punishments. Worldly happiness in comparison with that of the next world is very trifling. There is no end of time in the next world. Once poison begins to work, the physician cannot cure it. The sinner falls within the meaning of this verse I have put a bar in front of them and a bar behind them and covered them up so that they cannot see -36:9. Spiritual knowledge is the root and worldly knowledge is its branch.

It is now clear to you that faith has got many branches and when a man commits fornication, he does not remain a believer. The screen which falls on faith is also a branch. At the time of death, it will fall from the basic faith as a man advances towards death if he loses one limb but still has got life. There is no existence of faith without its branches. If there are branch without the root, they have got no existence. If there are branches, they indicate that there is the existence of the root, but the existence of the root only does not indicate the existence of the branches. So spiritual knowledge is the root and worldly knowledge is its branch. Both are linked together. One cannot go without the other.

Repentance is compulsory on the part of every Muslim in every condition as God says: O believers, be repentant to God all together so that you may get salvation 24:31. By this verse, all are called to be repentant. Tauba means to come near God from a distant path and to return from the path near the devil. Wisdom does not become perfect unless passions, angers and all other vile vices which are the instruments of the devil, and which misguide men are brought under full control. Wisdom becomes perfect at the advent of 40 years of age, and it begins after the age of maturity and takes its root at the age of seven years.

Passion, anger etc. are the soldiers of the devil and wisdom is the soldier of angels. When there is union of passion and wisdom, clash begins as one does not look at another with pleasure. They are opposed to each other and the difference between them is that of day and night or light and darkness. Sexual passion remains strong in youth before perfection of intellect. The soldiers of the devil come forward at that time. He who is a soldier of God has got his intellect shining. God says: The devil said: I will destroy the children of Adam except a few. If the intellect is firm, strong and perfect, its first duty is to control the sexual passion and greed and take the self towards divine service. This is the meaning of Tauba. There is no other meaning of Tauba except this. In other words, to control the passions and low desires of the self to return from the paths of the devil and to walk in the path of God. There is no such man whose sexual passion does not appear before his intellect. The evils of the devil appear before the natures of the angels and the former sits tight in heart before the latter. So, it is the duty of every man to return from the evil tendencies. A poet says:

Think not that Hinda alone is guilty of treachery, every chaste woman has got sin owing to her beauty.

Compulsory Tauba's Systematic Descriptions

Greed is engrained in human nature from birth. It is the natural passion of man and it is not possible to go against it. So whoever remains an infidel at the time of maturity, he should turn away from his infidelity. If he is a Muslim at the time of age and follows the Islam of his parents he should understand the meaning of Islam and turn towards real Islam as the Islam of his parents without understanding brings him no good. This is very hard and difficult. Tauba is directly compulsory on every man in every condition as he is not free from sins of his bodily limbs. There are traditions to show repentances and the wailings of the Prophets owing to their lapses. If any man is free from sin, still he is not free from thoughts of sins. If he is free from thoughts of sins, he is not free from the machinations of the devil as many impure thoughts keep him forgetful of God.

The object of Tauba is to return from sin. The Prophet said: The devil circles round my thoughts, for which I seek forgiveness to

God seventy times. When such is the condition of the Prophet, how is the condition of others?

Question. There is no doubt that the evil thought that. cross in mind are harmful and to be free from them is the sign of perfection. Perfection is not compulsory according to Shariat and to return to perfection, Tauba is necessary. So, what is the meaning that Tauba is compulsory under all circumstances.

Answer. Man is not free from greed from the beginning of his birth. So Tauba is not to give it up, but it is complete when past sins are enquired into, and one is repentant therefor. If a man follows his passion, a smoke rises in his heart as a result. When there is layer of smoke in heart, rust falls on it as mirror is filled up with smoke out of the breath of men. God says: Never, rather rust has fallen on their hearts for what they acquired. When rust is gathered on it, there falls therein seal, as a mirror becomes ugly if dust after dust falls on it. If it lasts long, it enters into the iron of the mirror and destroys it. If it is therefore not sufficient to give up only dust of passion in future but it is necessary also to remove the dusts already gathered. In order to see face in mirror it is not only necessary that there should be no smoke on it but all smokes and dusts gathered in the past on it must be removed. The smoke of sins and passions on heart should be removed by the light of divine worship. The following Hadis hints at that- "Do a good deed after an evil deed. It will wipe out the latter." It is only a good deed that can remove a bad deed according to the law of opposites. It is only cold that can remove heat. At first, heart remains pure. It assumes black colour for its opposite actions.

Meaning of Wajeb.

There are two meanings of Wajeb- (1) One meaning is compulsory actin which Shariat fixed as compulsory for all the people and the omission of which is a great sin, such as prayer, fast etc. (2) The second meaning of Wajeb is doing that duty which is outside the control of the ordinary men and with which search is made to be near the Almighty and to acquire the rank of the highest religious personalities. To make Tauba from the faults mentioned above is necessary to acquire that rank, as to make ablution is compulsory for a person who wishes to pray optional prayer to attain rank. He who remains satisfied being deprived of the rewards of optional prayer does not require an ablution, as eyes, hands and feet are not compulsory for a man to remain live. He who desires to be a full and perfect man, compulsorily requires these bodily organs.

So, the basic compulsory subjects are for the ordinary people as they take a man to basic salvation which is like living with a life. The additional things which lie behind this basic salvation bring fortune and perfection for which the prophets, saints and the friend of God strove hard and for which they gave up the pleasures of this worldly life. Even when Jesus Christ took a stone to be used as pillow for sleep the devil came and said: You have not given up the world for the next world. He said: Yes, how have you understood it? The devil said: You're using this stone as a pillow is included within the pleasure of the world. Why did you not place your head on the earth? Jesus Christ then threw away the stone and placed his head upon the ground. His throwing off the stone is his Tauba or return from that pleasure. To place the head upon the ground is not compulsory on the general public, but Jesus Christ did so to acquire the highest merit. Do you not notice that our Prophet threw off a cloth which he put on as it turned away his attention from prayer owing to its varied colours? It is not compulsory on his followers. He did it to acquire the highest rank. This is Tauba or return from a slip of mind. Do you notice that Hazrat Abu Bakr vomited out the milk which he had drunk as he came to know afterwards it was not earned lawfully? But it is no sin to eat an unlawful thing unknowingly and Shariat does not make compulsory to take it out from stomach. Think of those people who are the most informed of men regarding God, God's path and God's Marfat. You take great care that you may not be deceived by anybody in this world. What a great care you should take not to be deceived regarding the affairs of God and the next world.

Abu Solaiman Darani said: If a wise man does not weep during the rest of his life for defects in his divine service, he shall feel sorrow up to his death. Every moment of life or every breath is a treasure. There is no exchange of it as it is the basic thing. It will take you to everlasting fortune and rescue you from everlasting misfortune. If you lose it uselessly and negligently, you will be a great loser. If you spend it in sin, you will spoil you best treasure. If you do not weep for this loss, it will be for your mere ignorance. The danger of ignorance is more than that of all other things. All men are asleep. When they die, they are awake. Then their poverty will be disclosed to them.

A certain Aref said: If the angel of death informs a man that a moment only is left for his life, his grief rises to such a degree that in exchange of everything in the world he hopes to get some leisure to get an opportunity to make Tauba for his past misdeeds, but that is not to be. God says: Spend out of what I have given you before death comes to one of you, lest one of you says: O Lord, if you give me a little time, I will make charity and be one of the pious. God does not tarry a little for anybody when his time comes-63: 19. At the time of that catastrophe, his basic faith will totter and in this condition his life will end. If he has sent good deeds in advance, his life will go out with Tauhid. This is his Khatma- bil- Khair or end with good condition. If he is unfortunate, his life will go out in sorrows and anxieties. This is his bad end. For this reason, God says: Tauba is for those who commit sins out of ignorance and then soon repent, God will accept their repentance and He is All-knowing, the Wise. Tauba is not for those who commit sins till when death comes to one of them, he says: I now repent-4: 16. The Prophet says: Wipe out an evil by doing thereafter a good act.

Loqman said to his son: O darling make no delay in making Tauba as death comes suddenly. He who does not repent without delay lives in two dangers. One of the dangers is that the darkness of sins is congested in his heart to such an extent that in the end it is transformed into rust and seal is created and it can hardly be effaced. The second danger is that unless treatment is made of the disease, death is sure, and no delay can be made to wipe it out. There is therefore in Hadis: Most of the cries of the dwellers of Hell will be for salvation without delay. He who will be ruined will not be ruined without sorrow. So, his heart becomes black for the present and to secure it by divine service remains for the future. He remains in such condition up to his death and will return to God with unsound soul. There is no salvation except for a sound soul. Soul is a trust to man and life also is a trust to him. Whose ruins these trusts his matter is a subject of thoughts and anxieties.

A certain Aref said: God communicates by way of Ilham or inspiration two secret things. One of them is that when a man is born from his mother, He says to him: O My servant, I have taken you out to the world pure and clean and I have kept your life to Me as a trust and for that made you secure. I will look how you observe that trust and I will see how you meet Me. The second subject is that when his life goes out, God says: O My servant, what have you done with the trust I have kept with you? Have you preserved it till you have met Me? If you have preserved it, I will reward you in full. If you have preserved it, I will reward you in full. If you have ruined it, I will give you punishment. As God says: Fulfil My command and I will fulfil Mine. God says: Those who fulfil their trust and promise- 8: 23.

Condition of Acceptance of Tauba

Every sincere Tauba is accepted. Those who observe with the inner light and whose souls are bright know that every soul has been created pure and clean and every child has been created on natural attribute. But men have been polluting its purity and cleanliness with dirt and making it black with sins. They also know that these impurities on soul can be burnt by the fire of repentance and the light of good deeds can remove the darkness of dirt gathered on soul. The darkness of sins has got no power to live with the light of good deeds as the darkness of night cannot live with the light of day or as the dirt cannot remain, if a cloth is cleansed with soap, So God does not accept a soul polluted with sins. As a cloth being polluted by foul act can be cleansed with soap and warm water, so a soul being polluted with passion and greed can be purified of tears of eyes and fire or repentance. As a clean cloth is acceptable, so a soul being polluted with passion and greed can be purified of tears of eyes and fire of repentance. As a clean cloth is acceptable, so a pure and clean soul is acceptable to God. So, your soul should be cleansed and made pure. God says: The soul of one gets success which he has made pure.

One soul can recognize another soul. He Who does not know his soul, how can he know another soul? He who think that Tauba although sincere will not be accepted, is like a man who thinks that darkness will not go even if the sunrises or dirt will not go even if a cloth is washed by soap. But soap is not alone sufficient to remove dirt if it is gathered, layer over layer, on a thing Similar is the condition of sin if congested in soul. If one says by word of mouth "I repented" his word is like the word of a washerman who says by his tongue: I have washed this cloth. Such is the conciliation of a soul if no sincere repentance is made. This is sufficient for acceptance of Tauba for a man with deep insight. There are proofs of the Quran and Hadis to this effect.

God says: He it is who accepts Tauba from His servants and pardons sins. God says: I am Forgiving, Accepter of repentance. The Prophet said: God is more satisfied with the repentance of some of you. This satisfaction means acceptance of repentance, and this is the proof of acceptance of repentance. The Prophet said: God says: God also extends His hand of forgiveness towards one who is busy in commission of sins from night till daybreak and from daybreak till night. There are many repentances fit for acceptance which are not enquired into and there are many enquirers whose repentance is not accepted. The Prophet said: If you are engaged in the commission of sins which reach even heaven and then repent, God will accept it. He said: A man will enter paradise even after commission of sins. The companions asked: O Messenger of God, how can it be? He said: After commission of sins, he thinks how he can return from them. Thus, he will enter Paradise. Our Prophet said: Tauba expiates sins. The Prophet said: He who repents after commission of a sin is like one who has not committed it. A Negro slave once said to the Prophet: O Messenger of God, I am engaged in obscene deeds. Have I got any repentance? He said: Yes, you have. Then he returned from the sins, and said: O Messenger of God when I commit sin, does God see me? He said: Yes. Then the slave gave such a loud shriek that cost his life.

It is related that when God cursed the devil, he prayed to God for time, and He granted him time till the Resurrection Day. The devil then said: By the honour of your oath, I will not come out of the heart of a man till there is breath in him. God said: By My honour and glory. I will accept his repentance till there is life in his body. The Prophet said: A good deed removes an evil deed as water removes dirt.

Saying of Sages.

Sayed-bin Mosayyeb said regarding the event of revelation of this verse 'He is forgiving to those who repent' that a man repented after commission of a sin. Then he again committed that sin and again repented. Then God sent down the above verse. Fazil said: God said: Give good news to the sinners that if they repent, I will accept it. Give warning to the truthful that if I do justice in their case, I will punish them. Talqe-bin Habib said: Whatever duties man may do, God is much above that, but he should repent morning and evening. Abdullah-bin-Omar said: If a man after commission of sin gets afraid in mind, it is effaced from his record of deeds.

It is related that when a Prophet of Banu Israil committed a sin, God revealed to him: By My honour, if you commit sin another time, I will give you punishment. The Prophet said: O my lord, you are you and I am I. By your honour, if you do not save me, I may commit another sin. God then saved him. A certain sage said: If a man commits sins and then repents for his whole life, he shall enter paradise. The devil will then say: Alas, why have I thrown him into a sinful act? Ibn Mas'ud one day saw a man committing a sinful act. He asked him: Is there any repentance for this sin? Ibn Mas'ud first turned away from him and then looking towards him saw that he was shedding tears. He said to him: Paradise has got eight doors all of which will not be closed or opened. An angel will be entrusted with its not closing. So, act and act, don't be despaired. Abdur Rahman-bin-Abul Qasem said: We were discussing with Abdur-Rahman about repentance of the unbelievers and also about the verse of God: If they desist, He will forgive their past sins. He said: Hope that the condition of the Muslims will be good near God. I heard that the repentance of the Muslims after Islam will be like their acceptance of Islam. Abdullah-b-Salam you are narrating the following Hadis after hearing it from the Prophet or knowing it from the Book of God. When a man commits a sin and then repents for it soon, his sins drop down sooner than the twinkling of an eye. Hazrat Omar said: Sit with those who repent as their hearts are very soft.

It is related that a man of Banu Israil was engaged in commission of sins for twenty years after his divine service for twenty years. Thereafter when his look was drawn towards a beautiful woman, he said that his beard had grown grey. He felt grieved for this, and he prayed to God: O God, I did your service for 20 years and then committed sins for the last 20 years. If I turn to You now with repentance, will You accept me? Someone from the unseen said: When you had loved Me, I had loved you. When you gave Me up, I gave you up. When you committed sins again, I gave you a time. If you now return to Me, I will accept you. Zun-Nun said: There are such servants of God who saturate with the water of repentance the tree of sins when it grows. The fruits of sorrow and penance then come out of it. They are the givers of lessons, speakers and well-informed of God and His Apostle. They drink water from the cups of purity and remain patient for long in sorrows and difficulties. Then their minds become eager to sojourn in heavens, their thoughts enter into the mysteries of the spiritual world, they take shelter in the canopy of repentance and read then the records of sins. As a result, fear enters their hearts and reaches the utmost limit of renunciation embarking in the steps of God fear. They regard the bitterness of renunciation of the world as sweet and the roughness of bed as smooth. Even their glands of salvation and the staff of security grow strong, and their souls rise upwards and enter the garden of fortune. They make enjoyments in the sea of life and sing in the well despondency. They cross the bridge of passions and descend into the field of education, drink water in the tanks of wisdom, embark on the boat of peace and sail in the sea of security with the wind of salvation.

Tauba from Minor and Major Sins

Tauba means to give up sins. If a thing is not known, it is not possible to give it up. When Tauba is compulsory, the thing by which the condition of Tauba is reached is also compulsory.

Classes of Sin according to the Nature of Men

Man has got four natures. It is narrated regarding the wonderful qualities of the soul that the nature and conduct of man are many, but they can be limited within four natures, Godly-nature, devilish nature, beastly propensity, and propensity of ferocious beasts. The reason is that man has been created of different elements and every element has got its influences.

Firstly- Godly nature.

To boast, to take pride, to create, to love praise, to love honour and power, to wish to live forever, to wish to lord over all etc. are the Godly qualities in a man. (2) Secondly, the devilish natures are hatred, rebellion, fraud, cheating, disturbance, and all kinds of evils. (3) Thirdly, beastly propensities like greed for satisfaction of stomach, fornication, theft, eating of the property of orphans etc. (4) Fourthly, propensities of ferocious beasts, out of which grow the evils of anger, attack, rebuke, killing, etc. They come in order. Firstly, beastly propensities remain strong and then propensities of ferocious beasts come. When these two propensities unite, they make intellect subservient to practice cheating, fraud. This is also the nature of the divine at last, the Godly qualities become strong - greed for name and fame, greed for honour, desire for lordship over people etc. These are the roots of sins all fountains. Sins flow from these fountains into the bodily limbs. Some sins fall in mind, such as infidelity, hypocrisy, will for doing harm to men. Some sins fall in eyes and ears, some in tongue, some in stomach and organs of passion, some in hands and feet and some in the whole body.

Second class of sins.

Sins come from breach of duty towards God and men. The sins arising out of the breach of duties towards God are to give up prayer, fasting and other compulsory duties. The major sins arising from breach of duties towards men are to give up Zakat, to kill a man unjustly, to misappropriate the properties of others, to destroy the rights of others. It occurs in connection with life, properties, religion, name, and fame. The punishment of sins for breach of duty towards men is sure and the sins of breach of duties towards God are expected to be pardoned. There is in the tradition: There are three matters-one matter is fit to be pardoned, one matter is not fit to be pardoned and one matter is fit to be given up. The matter which is to be pardoned is the breach of duty towards God. The matter which is not fit to be pardoned is to set up partnership with God. The matter which is fit to be given up is the breach of rights of men. There is no pardon of that sin unless the owner of right forgives him.

Third class of sins.

There is difference of Third opinion with regard to major sins. Sins are divided into major and minor. Some say there is no such distinction as major and minor sins, rather whatever is done against the order of God is a major sin. This argument is weak as God says: If you give up the major sin of which you have been prohibited, I shall compensate your minor sins for you and cause you to enter an honourable place-4:31. God says: Those who give up major sins and indecent acts except those evil thoughts which arise suddenly in mind. The Prophet said: Five times of prayer and prayers from one Juma to another compensate the sins in between them if the major sins are given up. The Prophet said: To set up partnership with God, to be disobedient towards parents, to kill and to break the promise are major sins. The companions differed and fixed the major sins as four, seven, nine or eleven. Ibn Mas'ud said that their number is four, Hazrat Ibn Omar said that their number is seven. Hazrat Abdullah bin-Amr said that they are nine. Hazrat Ibn Abbas said that they are seventy and the nearest of them is seven. A certain sage said: The sin for which there is the fire of Hell as a punishment is major sin. Some say that the number of major sins is not known as the blessed night of the auspicious moment of Juma is not known. Abu Taleb Makki said that they are seventeen. He said: I have gathered then from Hadis and from Ibn Abbas, Ibn Mas'ud, Ibn Omar and other companions. Out of them, four have connection with mind-(1) to set up partnership with God, (2) to do a sin repeatedly, (3) to be despaired of the mercy of God, and (4) not to fear the punishment of God. Four have got connection with tongue-(1) to depose falsely, (2) to slander a chaste woman, (3) to break promise, and (4) to make sorcery. Three have got connection with stomach- (1) to drink intoxicant, (2) to eat the property of an orphan, and (3) to enjoy interest with knowledge. Two have got connection with the sexual organ-(1) to commit fornication, and (2) to cohabit with boys. Two have got connection with hands-(1) to kill, and (2) to steal. One has got connection with leg-to flee away from fighting with the infidels. One has got connection with the whole body, to be disobedient to parents.

Comparison makes a sin major or minor. A thing becomes bigger in comparison with a small thing. Again, a thing is called small when compared to a bigger thing than it. If a man lies with a strange woman in the same bed, his lying is greater than looking at her and smaller than fornication with her. Sins are divided into three-(1) sins which are known to be major, (2) sins known to be minor, and (3) sins which Shariat has not fixed to be major or minor. Imam Ghazali said: The thing which stands as an impediment to God's knowledge is a major sin and the thing which ruins life and ruins the means of livelihood is a major sin.

Major sins have got three stages.

(1) The thing which stands as an impediment in heart for preservation of Marfat, and the thing which stands as an

impediment to the acquisition of God's knowledge or knowledge of the Prophet is infidelity disbelief which is the greatest of all major sins. Ignorance is the screen between God and His Servants and knowledge is the means of doing good deeds. In accordance with the measure of knowledge about Him, nearness is gained and in accordance with ignorance about Him, there is distance from Him. Ignorance has got another name named infidelity. He who has got knowledge of Him cannot remain safe and cannot be also despaired. He travels in these new stages which have got connection with God's attributes and actions. According to the Quran, there are three classes of sins (1) what are known as major sins in the Quran, (2) what are known as minor sins in the Quran, and (3) the sins which have got doubt of being called major sins.

(2) With regard to the second stage of major sins, it is the impediment to save life, as knowledge of God can be acquired if there is life. So to commit suicide is a major sin, but lower than infidelity. To cut off hands and feet and the thing which leads to sudden death are major sins. So also, fornication and unnatural cohabitation are major sins as in a case of this nature there is no fixation of lineage and cutting the existence of man.

(3) The third stage has got connection with properties, as properties are the means of livelihood. It is not permissible for men to earn them arbitrarily, such as theft, decoity, misappropriation of money. In four ways, properties may be misappropriated. The first way is to take property secretly or by stealing. The second way is to eat the properties of an orphan which is also done secretly. The third way is to

misappropriate property by false deposition. The fourth way is to get deposited property by false oath.

Punishment and Reward in the Next World

Know, O readers, that this world is visible material world, and the next world is invisible spiritual world. The meaning of this world is your condition before your death and the next world is your condition after your death. The name of near condition is this world and of distant condition is the next world. Examples are the only means of describing the next world as we are now living in this world. God says: I have given these examples for men and none but the wise appreciate them. The reason is that this material world is like a dream in comparison with the next world. The Prophet said: 'Men are in sleep. They will wake up after their death'. What occurs in wakeful state is not expressed in dream except in examples which are subject to interpretation. Similarly, what will occur in the next world in wakeful state is not clear without examples of sleep of this world.

Once a man came to Ibn Sirin and said: (1) I saw in dream as if there is a seal in my hand with which I am giving impression in the faces and places of shame. He said: It seems you are a Muzzen and will proclaim before dawn in the month of Ramzan. He said: You have spoken the truth. (2) Another man came and said: I saw in dream that I am pouring olive oil on my head. He said: Enquire into the condition of your slave if you have got any. It seems that she is your mother and was a prisoner in your childhood, as the root of oil is olive tree and it returned to its root. After examination, it was found that she was his mother and that she was taken a prisoner in his childhood. (3) Another man said to him: I saw in dream that I am dressing the neck of a swine with a necklace of emeralds. He said: It means that you are teaching wisdom to undeserving persons. The interpretation of dream occurs in such a way from the beginning to the end. The Prophet used to speak to men by way of illustrations and examples as they were ordered to speak to men according to the degree of the intelligence of me men. The intelligence of men is as it were confined to the mist of dream. Nothing is expressed to men who see anything in dream without examples. When they die, they wake up and understand that the illustrations are true. For this reason, the Prophet said: The heart of man is situated within two fingers of the Merciful. Nobody except the wise can understand it. The fools take it literally and understand this that God has got hands and fingers, from which He is pure. Similarly, the Prophet said: God created Adam according to His image. They understand it as material figure and colour. So, they construct the images of God, while He is pure of all forms. Similarly, the affairs of the next world are explained by illustrations. Many take it literally true. The Prophet said: On the Resurrection Day, death will be presented in the form of a goat without hairs, and it will be slaughtered. Some say it is a false Hadis as death has got no body and goat has got a body. It is just like the saying of a man: I dream that a goat was taken to me, and it was slaughtered. It means that the epidemic disease of the town was slaughtered.

The nutshell of this talk is that the angel who is entrusted with dream presents to human soul in sleep which is written in the Guarded Tablet. He informs by illustration as a sleeping man cannot understand it except by illustration. It comes true and its meaning is correct. The illustration that death will be presented in the next world in the form of a goat without hair is that after the first death of a man, there will be no other death, as a slaughtered animal is not expected to come again. There is in the Quran: 'Be and it comes into being'. This is explained as unlimited power. It is not possible to explain the punishments of sins and the rewards of virtues without illustrations. We say that on the Resurrection Day, men will be of different classes and their ranks will be also different, as in the world there is difference of fortunes and misfortunes. The next world does not keep this world separate as the Conductor of the next world and this world is one without having any partner.

Man will be divided into Four Classes in the Next world.

One class are for destruction, one class for punishment, one class for salvation, and one class for success. The following is the illustration in this world. A certain powerful king in order to establish his kingdom on a firm basis kills some people and they are the destroyed people. He punishes some persons for a certain time, but he does not kill them. They are those who receive punishment. He releases some persons who are recipients of salvation. He gives rewards to some persons who are successful. If the king is just, he classes his subjects on the basis of justice only. He does not kill except those who deny his sovereignty. He does not punish except those who have got defects in their service to him. He does not release except those who admit the kings rank and positions. He does not give rewards except to those who spend their lives in his service.

There is also difference in the rewards of those who get rewards according to the extent of their service and help to the king. Similarly, those who are destroyed get punishment according to the extent of their mischief and wrongdoing. Some are killed outright, the hands and feet of some are cut off and then killed. Then understand that in the next world, also the people will be divided into different classes. Some will be destroyed; some will get salvation and enter the abode of peace, and some will receive rewards. The nearest persons will receive rewards. The rewarded persons will be of different classes, some will enter the paradise of Eden, some will enter the paradise of Maoa, some Ferdous. Similarly, those who will receive punishment will be also of different classes. Some will be given slight punishment some will be given punishment from one thousand years to seven thousand years. Similarly, those who will be destroyed will be deprived of God's mercy.

Stages of Those Who Will Meet with Destruction.

The person who will meet with destruction are those who will be deprived of God's mercy. They are like those persons whom a king kills on account of their opposition and who have been deprived of king's mercy. Those who deny the existence of God, those who are engaged in worldly pursuits and those who disbelieve God, His Prophets and His books are included within this class. Fortune in the next world means gaining nearness of God and meeting with Him. This nearness cannot be gained without knowledge of God. This knowledge arises out of faith and there is its corroboration. Those who deny the existence of God are the disbelievers deprived of God's mercy. The lovers of God said: We don't fear the fire of Hell, nor do we hope for the black- eyed Hurs. Our only hope is meeting with our Lord and the lifting of screen from us. They say: He who serves God in exchange of getting something is dishonourable, deprived and subject of hatred. He serves God only to get Paradise or to ward off punishment of Hell, but a lover of God serves Him only to meet with Him. Fire burns only the body but the fire of separation burns both the body and soul. The fire of separation is enkindled by God which rises up to the heart. A poet said: - Fire of separation in a lover's heart is high and severe.

Fire of Hell in comparison is trifling and like snow.

He on whom the fire of love is enkindled walks upon fire and runs over the bamboo points and cannot feel pangs owing to the urge of love. You will see an angry man fight even after receiving wounds but not feeling any pain.

Second stage.

Those who will get punishment. They are the people who have got faith but have got shortcomings for neglect to act according to it. The root of faith is Tauhid or faith in the unity of God. He who follows his passion accepts it as his deity and not God. He is not a true unitarian. God says: Say God and then leave them in their useless talks. The real meaning of this is: Give up everything except God. God says in its support: 'Those who say God is our Lord' and then they firmly stand on it-60: 30. This means that this is the straight path without which Tauhid is not perfect. This path is slenderer than hair and sharper than sword. This is like the bridge of the next world. Man strays away little or more from this straight path as he is not free from the propensities of nature. He goes away from Tauhid in proportion to his going away from this path. This occurs for two reasons-strength of faith and its weakness and following low desires more or little. God said: There is nobody among you who will not come to it (Hell). It is a decree of God. God said: Then I will give those who are God-fearing salvation, and I will make the sinners turned down- 19: 71.

The Prophet said: Some persons will be taken out of Hell after one thousand years, and they will cry: O Merciful. Hearing this Hadis, Hasan Basari said: Alas! had I been one of those persons! It is in the tradition that the man who will come out last of all from Hell will come out of it after seven thousand years. Some will come out of it like lightning. Some will remain in Hell for seven thousand years. So, there are days, weeks, months, and years within this period. Punishment will be meted out different times for different persons. There will be also different kinds of punishment as a king mete it out to his subjects. He fines some persons, whips some, confiscates the properties of some, deports some, beats some, kills the children of some, takes the wives of some as slaves, chops; off the nose, hands, and feet of some. Similarly, there will be different kinds of punishment in the next world. The greater the sins, the greater the punishments. There are several kinds of punishment for several kinds of sins. Those who are adept in soul give proof of the above by the Quranic verses: God says: Your Lord is not an oppressor of His servants. He says: Every soul will be given today what it earned- 12: 286. He says: Man shall have nothing but what he strives for. He says: He shall see even and atom of good he does, and he shall see an atom of evil he does 99: 8.

There will be justice and no injustice, but the scale of pardon and forgiveness will be heavy, as the Prophet said that God had said: My compassion overcome My wrath. God says: If you do a good deed, God will increase it and give you abundant rewards from Him. It seems that whose establishes his faith firm, keeps away from all major sins, does all the compulsory duties and does not do except minor sins and even these also not repeatedly, his punishment will be confined only within accountings, because when his accounts will be taken, his virtues will be heavier than his sins. There is in

Hadis that the prayer for five times, Juma prayer and the fast of Ramzan expiate the sins committed during the period. Similarly, if the major sins are given up, the minor sins are expiated, therefore.

Different stages of the Fortunate

To enter the highest Paradise or to live near the fortunate one depends upon faith of different kinds. Faith is of two kinds-blind faith of the ordinary people and faith born out of direct inner sight which is gained with the expansion of breast by the help of God's light. By virtue of this faith, the knowledge of everything appears to him and it becomes clear to him that everything will return to God as there is no existence of anything except that of God, His attributes, and His actions. These are they who will live near God and reside in the highest Ferdous.

There are different classes of these fortunate persons. Some will be advancing and some retracing. Their rank will vary according to the variance of their degree of knowledge of God. There are many stages of God's lovers as there are many steps of knowledge of God. There is no end of the depth of the ocean of Marfat and there is no such person who can cross that ocean. The divers according to their strength and the strength given to them by divine order can divine therein. There is no end of the path towards God. So, there is no limit to the stage of those persons who walk in the path of God. He who has got better faith is also one of the fortunate people. His rank is lower than that of the fortunate Prophets. The highest rank of the fortunate men of blind faith is near the rank of the near ones. The man who gives up major sins, does the compulsory duties, stands upon the five pillars of Islam, utters Kalema Shahadat by tongue and heart, performs pilgrimage, gets this rank. He who committed major sins and neglected to do other compulsory duties but made sincere repentance before his death, will live with that person who has not committed these sins. A washed cloth is like the cloth which has got no dirt from the beginning. If he dies before repentance, his time of death will be fraught with dangers. Blind faith at the first tempest of slight doubt is shaken at the root. He who is wise with deep insight keeps himself away from this danger at the time of death.

He who continues to commit sins for as many days as he likes will get proportionate punishment therefor. He who does heinous sins will get severe punishment. He who does different kinds of sins will get different kinds of punishment, he will not come near the rank of the fortunate ones. Those who are agnostics with deep insight will live in the highest Paradise. There is in Hadis: He who will be taken last out of Hell will be given space ten times of this world. If the area of this world is one thousand miles, don't think he will be given space ten times of one thousand miles. This is like the saying of the man: I have given one who has taken my one camel ten camels. This means that if the price of a camel is ten dinars, he was given hundred dinars. The Prophet said: Paradise is situated in heaven. It appears that heaven is in this world. So how can Paradise be situated in the world ten times of this world? It should not be taken literally.

Causes of Disasters on Religious People

The Prophet said: Be kind on three persons- (1) a learned man among the illiterate, (2) a rich man among the poor, and (3) an honourable man among the dishonourable persons. For this reason, the Prophets are the recipients of kindness among his followers as they suffered owing to the short intelligence of their followers.

Those are tests from God for their examination and come from God according to destiny. For this reason, the Prophet said: Disasters fell upon the Prophets, then on the friends of God, and then on the religious persons, like them. Disaster came upon the Prophet Ayub, so also on Noah as he was tested for a group of people. Whenever the harsh word of a person gave the Prophet sorrow, he used to say: God showed mercy on my brother Moses who had to suffer much more hardship than this, but he remained patient. When the Prophets were not secure from the enmity of the oppositionists and when the friends of God and the learned were not saved from the fools, the friends of God are not free from dangers and difficulties. They are also tested by trials. They are driven out of towns and cities. They are blamed before the ruling power and some men attribute to them infidelity. The followers of Marfat are known to the illiterate as fools.

When you have become aware of the truth of this subtle matter, believe then in the following words of the Prophet. The man who will come out last of all from Hell will get space ten times of the world. Be careful of believing only what your external sense organs can catch. If you only believe that you will be an ass with two legs as you have got five senses, and an ass also has got five senses. The Latifa or the subtle matter for which you are distinguished from an ass was presented to the heavens, earth, and mountains but they refused to accept it and they were afraid of it. It is not of the material world and is outside of the world governed by five senses. It is included within the spiritual world in which no lower animal can enter. He who neglects this valuable thing and keeps it as useless, ruins himself. So don't include yourself within those who forget God. He who does not know except the knowledge gained by five senses, forgets God as God is not to be known only by the five senses and God makes one forgetful of his soul who forgets God. He misuses the trust placed in him by God. He is worse than a beast, as a heart gets salvation after its death but the trust in him after his death will be returned to him.

Nobody except a believer in the unity of God, will come out of Hell. By unity of God, I don't mean only utterance of "There is no deity but God" as tongue is of this material world and it will not get benefit except in this material world. The essence of Tauhid is within mind. What is known to be true will do benefit. Tauhid becomes perfect when it is known that nothing happens except by the command of God. Its sign is not to get angry with any person, as the cause of an action is nobody but God. So, Tauhid is divided into different classes. There are persons whose Tauhid is firm like a rock. There are persons whose Tauhid is like the weight of a seed. They will nevertheless be taken out of Hell. The Prophet said: He who has got faith to the weight of a seed will be taken out of Hell.

Most persons believing in Tauhid will go to Hell on account of their oppression on the people. A man may have mountain like virtues, but the oppressed people will stand before him. He destroyed the honour of some persons, misappropriated money of others, beat and assaulted others, and backbited others. They will be given compensation from his virtues. When his virtues will end, the angels will say: O Lord, this man has finished his virtues, but there are other claimants. God will say: Add their sins with his sins and throw him into Hell. So, he will enter Hell for the sins of others and the oppressed persons will get the virtues of the oppressors and will go to Paradise. It is related that one of the friends of Ibn Jala backbited him. When his friends sought his pardon, he said: I will not forgive him. There is no virtue in my record of deeds like his virtues. How can I efface it? He also said: Backbiting is a sin for my friend, but a virtue for me. I wish to embellish my record of deeds therewith.

A Physician thinks that a certain patient will die, and no medicine will bring his cure. He thinks of another patient who will be cured. But it is seen that the former patient has recovered, and the latter had died. This is the mystery of God and outside the scope of the knowledge of man. The salvation and success in the next world are just like that They have got secret causes outside human knowledge. For this reason, we should forgive the guilty and not express anger on the virtuous. God says: God does not oppress anybody-21: 47. He says: God does not oppress anybody to the extent even of an atom. He says: Man does not earn anything except by his efforts. His efforts will be considered- 53: 38. He says, everybody is responsible for his action -6: 115. He Says: When they were misguided, He closed their minds. He says: When they changed their conditions, God changed their condition. God says: God does not change the condition of a people till they change their own condition. These verses are clear to those who are adept in the knowledge of soul just as a person sees anything with his eyes. Eyes in some cases commit mistakes, as they see near what lies distant and see little what is big. But the eye of heart or soul cannot commit mistake. To this effect, the Quran says: The heart has not taken as false what it has seen- 53:11.

Persons who get salvation.

Salvation means security without fortune or success. Those who got Salvation did not do divine service and they did not get rewards although they were secure of punishment. They are like boys among the infidels or deranged of brain. They are like those persons who did not receive invitation to accept Islam and lived in unknown places. They have no knowledge of God and no actions of religion. They have got no such sin as can keep them away from God. They are neither the inmates of Paradise nor of Hell. They will remain in a place between Paradise and Hell called A'raf or elevated place.

Rewarded persons.

They are not blind believers but are cognisant of God with deep insight. They are the near ones and will get rewards beyond description. God says: Nobody knows what consoling rewards to the eyes are reserved for them. The Prophet said that God says: I have prepared for My righteous servants such reward as no eye has seen, no ear has heard and no heart of a man has conceived. The matter of enquiry of the Arefs or agnostics is to get that condition which no other man in the world can appreciate. They don't want palaces, beautiful damsels, milk, honey, wine, ornaments of paradise, but they desire for Divine sight the less of which they will not be satisfied. This is the end of fortune and tests. Hazrat Rabia was asked: What is desirable in Paradise? She said: To get Neighbour and then a house. These persons are engrossed in the love of the Master of the house and not of its embellishments. This condition is called Fana fillah.

When a Minor Sin turns into a Major Sin?

1. The first cause

Is that any minor sin if done repeatedly turns into a major sin. It is therefore said: If a minor sin is committed repeatedly, it does not remain a minor sin. If a major sin is committed and then there is repentance for it, it does not remain a major sin. In short, if a person commits a major sin and then refrains from it and does not do it again, it is expected to be forgiven more than a minor sin which he commits repeatedly. For instance, if water falls repeatedly on a stone, there falls a sign thereon but if once only water is flown on it there will be no sign thereon. For this reason, the Prophet said: A good deed though trifling is good if done always. Anything small, it done repeatedly, brings good, and anything great, if not done always, is less beneficial to the progress of soul and its purity. Similarly, a minor sin done repeatedly turns into a major sin and its influence to blacken a soul is great. A great sinner first of all commits minor sins and then jumps into a major sin. A fornicator rarely commits fornication without doing some deeds of love. A person rarely kills a man without first cherishing hatred and enmity for him. So, before every major sin, minor sins are committed. If minor sins are committed throughout life, they cannot be expected to be forgiven, but if a major sin is committed suddenly, it is expected to be forgiven.

2. The second cause

Is to belittle sin. When a person thinks a sin great, he humbles himself before the Merciful. When he humbles himself, he becomes great. The influence of sin then does not fall in his heart to a great extent. If a sin is thought as insignificant, it is understood that the sin has cemented love with the heart and for this reason its influence on heart is great. Hadis: 'A believer considers a sin hanging like a rock on his head, while a hypocrite considers a sin trifling like a bee which passes over his nose. A believer takes sin as great and also thinks a minor sin as great. God sent revelation to a certain Prophet: Don't see the trifling nature of a present but look to the nobility of the giver of the present. Don't think sin as small but look whom you are opposing by this sin. An Aref said from this angle of vision: There is no minor sin. Every opposition to God is a great sin. A certain companion said to his successors: You commit such sins which are thinner than your eyelash, but we regarded them as causes of ruin at the time of the Prophet. The companions regarded the minor sins as great. For this reason, the ignorant people do not think a minor fault as sin, while the learned consider it as a major sin. This matter bypasses a blind man but not one having eyes.

3. Third cause

To get pleasure in sin. If pleasure is found by committing a minor sin, it turns into a major sin. Whenever the pleasure of a minor sin is great, it turns into a major sin. Even there are persons who take pride after commission of such minor sins. For instance, one may say: Have you seen how I have injured his honour and how I have made him a fool?

4. The fourth cause

Is to think a minor sin as trifling as it met with no punishment. God has kept his sin secret and as such He keeps patience at it and gives him time to repent and to seek forgiveness. If the sinner neglects it, the minor sin turns into a major sin. The sinner is unaware that God gives him time disliking it. He thinks that as the sin does not meet with punishment, God was kind to him. This is not kindness of God, but it is His plan and trick, and nobody can be secure of his sin. God says: They think that God may give punishment for what they say. Hell is sufficient for them. They will enter therein. How bad is this place of entry.

5. The fifth cause

Is that if a sin is disclosed, it turns into a major sin. If a man commits a sin and then discloses it or if he commits it in presence of others, he lifts the screen which God has thrown upon his sin and gives encouragement to others by his sin. If others hear of his sins or see his actions of sins, these are also acts of sin. It appears from this that one sin creates another sin, and hence his guilt increases. There is in Hadis that the sins of all, except those who disclose their sins, deserve to be forgiven. A certain sage said: Don't commit sin. If by chance a sin is committed, don't commit another sin by giving encouragement to others. For this reason, God says: The hypocrite male and hypocrite female are friends to each other. They enjoin evil deeds and prohibit good deeds.

6. Sixth cause.

The minor sin of a learned man turns into a major win. The reason is that the people follow the learned men. If anyone for them commits a minor sin, the people also commit it as they follow him. If a learned man puts on silk dress or a gold ring, enjoys the doubtful properties of others frequently, goes to the darbar of a ruling authority, learns such a learning with which he wishes to argue with others and seeks name and fame, these will turn into major sins if the people follow his actions. Even after his death, these evils continue in the world. Thanks to the learned man with whose death there is the end of his sin. There is in Hadis that whose introduces a bad custom, his sin and the sins of those who follow him devolve on him and his sins will never be reduced a little. God says: We shall record what they sent in advance and their signs. The meaning of these signs is what remains of their actions after they are done and what remains with its doer. Hazrat Ibn Abbas said: Woe to the learned man who follows in his bad action. If the slips he repents but the people hear it and travel therewith in the country. A certain sage said: The slip of a learned man is like the break of a boat which capsizes with those who are on board of it.

There is a book of Banu Israil that a learned man misguided the people by his innovation. Then he repented and began to do good deeds for a pretty long time. God revealed to His Prophet to tell him: If his sin would have been confined between him and me, I would have forgiven him. How can I forgive one who misguides my servants? I will throw him into Hell along with them. It appears from this that the affairs of the learned man are very serious. They have got the duty of giving up sin and the duty of concealing it. As their sins are increased, their virtues also are increased, as the people follow them in both their actions. If a learned man gives up the enjoyments of the world and attachment of the world and remains satisfied with little food and drink and old clothes, gets virtues like the virtues of those who followed him in these affairs. If he does the contrary and remains attached to the enjoyments of the world only, he becomes the cause of these evils.

Conditions of Tauba

Tauba means repentance and determination for not doing the same again. Knowledge, repentance, and determination are the conditions of Tauba. Repentance is the name of grief that comes as a result of loss of a dear thing. It has got many signs and pangs of mind and sorrow, shedding tears, weeping for a long time, living in cares and anxieties. What thing other than sins shows path to punishment? Who else except God and His Apostle is the giver of true news? There is in Hadis: Live with those who repent, as their minds are very soft. There is a story of Banu Israil that a man committed a sin and then repented and remained engaged for many years in divine service but still his repentance was not accepted. The Prophet of the time was asked about the acceptance of his Tauba and God revealed to him: By My honour and glory if their inmates of heaven and earth make intercession for him, I will not except his repentance as the pleasure of sin still lies within his mind.

Question. Mind naturally turns towards sinful acts. Why should there be taste of bitterness?

Answer. Someone drinks honey mixed with poison and gets taste at the time of drinking, but thereafter he suffers for long after he falls ill, his hairs fall down, and his limbs get swollen. If thereafter honey mixed with poison is given to him, although he is then hungry and has got a great desire to enjoy sweet things, he will hesitate in drinking that honey. The bitterness of sin is like that to a repentant. So, the pleasure of every sin is like the taste of honey, but there is poison in it. Without this belief, Tauba cannot be sincere. When this belief becomes difficult his repentance cannot be sincere. Believe that there is ruinous poison in every sin as you believe firmly that poison is ruinous.

Determination or firm will.

The firm will which comes out of repentance is the will of enquiry. It has got connection with the present, future and past. Regarding its connection with the present, it gives advice to one to give up every sin, every prohibited thing and to do all compulsory duties. With regard to its connection with the past, it enquires into omission of duties. With regard to its connection with future, it advices him to take care, so that there should be no further omission of compulsory duties and doing divine service always and giving up sins up to death.

The condition of sincere Tauba is that one should prepare for correction of past misdeeds. From the day of emission of semen up to the present time, take account of all omissions and commissions and rectify these, observe the omitted prayers, pay the dues of Zakat, and do other duties like fasting and pilgrimage. If you could not have fasted in Ramzan, you should keep them. If you had means of going to pilgrimage and you now had not done it, do it and if you cannot do it now owing to poverty, you should try to do it or else you will be a sinner. If you die before making pilgrimage, you will die as a sinner as the Prophet said: He who dies without making pilgrimage may die if he wishes as a Christian, or if he wishes as a Jew. Regarding other sins enquire about those committed up to date by your ears, eyes, tongue, stomach, hands, feet, and sexual organ, and try to repent for them and remove the wrongs you have done to others by the commission of sins. Repent sincerely for the sins for breach of duties towards God. Take account of all the sins from maturity up to date and do one good deed in place of sin. The Prophet said: Fear God and do a good deed after an evil and it will efface it. God says: Good deeds remove the bad ones-11: 114. Your object will be to give up every sin as harmful as poison.

Sin is darkness, and virtue are light. As darkness can be removed by light, so also sin can be removed by virtue. This is the easy way for effacing sins, as a thing can be destroyed by its opposite thing. Love for the world is the root of all sins. The Prophet said: There are some kinds of sins which are expiated only by cares and anxieties. The Prophet also said: When the sins of a man become too much and there remains no such good deeds which can expiate his sins God admits in his minds cares and anxieties which expiate his sins.

Question. Man's cares and anxieties generally arise in connection with his properties, children, name, and fame. Can they be expiation of sins?

Answer. To love the above things are sins but if he is deprived of those things, his sins are expiated. It is narrated that Gabriel once came to Joseph in his prison. The latter asked him: How far have you burdened my old father with sorrows and anxieties? Gabriel said: He has been given sorrows to the extent of grief of a mother who lost one hundred sons. Joseph said: What rank will he get near God, therefore? Gabriel said: The rank of one hundred martyrs."

Breach of duties towards the people.

In this matter also you have some duty towards God as prohibited the people from oppression. So far this breach of duty he should be penitently sincere to Him and promise not to do it again in future. Be kind to a man whom you have oppressed. Return to him his properties if you have taken them unjustly. Praise one whose honour you have destroyed. Speak good of your neighbour whom you have backbitten. These will not save you unless you refrain from doing wrong to others. If you have done harm to the life or honour of a man or given trouble to his heart, you have oppressed him. If you have killed a person out of mistake, give blood money to his heirs.

It is reported that Maez-bin-Malek came to the Prophet and said: O Messenger of God, I have committed adultery and I have oppressed my soul. So, purify me. This is my wish." The Prophet turned him back. On the following day, he came again to the Prophet and said as above. He turned him back for the second time. When he said this for the third and fourth time, he passed orders for his punishment. A pit was dug for him, and he was put therein and stoned to death. There were two parties over this affair, some said "He has been ruined." Some said: "There is no other sincere Tauba like his. " The Prophet said: "He has repented in such a way that if it would have been divided among the people, it would have been sufficient for them. "

On another day, one Gamedi woman came to the Prophet and said: "I have committed adultery, purify me." The Prophet turned her away. On the following day she came again to the Prophet and said: "O Messenger of God, why did you turn me away? You have thought that as you have turned away Maez, you will also turn me away. By God, I have conceived." The Prophet said: "Go away till you give birth to a child." Immediately after the child was born, she came to the Prophet with the child putting on a torn cloth and said: "My child is born." The Prophet said: "Go and suckle it, till it comes to an end." When the suckling ended, she came to the Prophet with the boy in whose hand there was a piece of bread. She said: "O Prophet of God, I have finished suckling and now he has been taking food." The Prophet then handed over the boy to a Muslim. A pit was dug up to her breast and the Prophet then passed order to stone her to death. Hazrat Khalid- bin-Walid threw a piece of stone on her head which gave out a streak of blood which fell on his face, and he was rebuking her. The Prophet heard it, rebuked him for it and said:" Stop, O Khaled, one in whose hand there lies my life, she has made such a Tauba that if a collector of Zakat in excess of limit makes such a Tauba, his Tauba will be accepted. She was then buried after funeral prayer. If the money of somebody was taken by force or there was a breach of trust or the wages of a labourer were not paid or paid less, it is incumbent together information of these things from the time of maturity up to date and to pay their just dues.

Regarding property.

If the owner is known, it is incumbent on him to return it to him. If the owner is not known, it should be given in charity. If you have given trouble to the mind of anybody, seek pardon from him. The Prophet said: One of your predecessors killed 99 persons and asked: Who is the wisest man in the world? When a saint was mentioned to him, he came to the saint and said, "O saint I have killed 99 persons. Will my Tauba be accepted?" The saint said "Your Tauba will not be accepted." Hearing this he killed the saint and filled up his number of murders to one hundred. Then he enquired of the greatest learned man in the world. when his name was mentioned, he came to him and asked him: I have killed one hundred persons. Will my Tauba be accepted? He said: "Yes, your Tauba will be accepted. What is the reason of its not being accepted? There you will find some persons engaged in divine service. Do divine service along with them and don't come to your native place as the land is not good." When the man was halfway to that land, he breathed his last.

With each other regarding his case. The angel of mercy said, "He has repented and turned his face towards God." The angel of punishment said: "He did never do any good deed. When another angel in the form of a man came there, they took him as an umpire to settle the matter. He said: Fix the distance between the two paths and he will get the path which is nearest to him. They measured the two paths and found that he crossed the path of repentance more than the other path. Then the angel of mercy took him with him, and he was forgiven.

Determination in Future

Firm determination shall have to be taken, so that sins are not committed in future. Hold firm connection with God, take such firm determination that no such sin is committed in future. Be like such a patient who knows in his illness that the eating of fruits will do harm and for that he takes such firm resolve that till he is cured he will not take fruits again. Till such firm resolve is made, there will be no Tauba. Your Tauba will not be perfect till you keep separate from you greed, keep silence, eat less and sleep less and take firm precautions in eating lawful things, as eating of unlawful things is the root of all sins. He who cannot give up greed in foods and drinks, his eating of lawful things and giving up of doubtful things are not sufficient. A certain sage said: "If a man repents for his sins and keeps patience for seven years, he will not again come to that sin."

Question. What is your opinion regarding (1) a person who forgets his sins and does not think of it, and (2) a person who remembers his sins and does not forget it?

Answer. One section of the learned men say that Tauba means keeping sins in front. Another section say that it means to forget sins. To us, these two opinions are both true according to circumstances. There are many ways to go to God, some near and some distant. To keep sins in front and to remember them is good for a beginner in the path of religion, as in case he forgets them, his repentance will not increase, and for that his will to walk in the way of God will not be so strong. If he remembers his sins, his sorrows will increase, and he will fear to commit them again. The above person is better than a careless person, but it is more injurious to a sojourner for religion as in the case of journey remembrance of sin is an impediment. Rather he should not deviate from the straight path of religion. In case sexual passion becomes strong, if the sin of fornication is remembered, it is injurious and to forget it is better. The Prophet said: "Be careful, I commit no mistake, but I am thrown to a mistake so that I may understand it." In another narration, I am made to forget in order to establish a way of life. The Prophet talked to men according to their intelligence. When Hazrat Hassan took some dates in his mouth to eat, the Prophet said "Kakh Kakh" meaning vomit it. He did not then understand the word "Vomit the dates" as he was then too young. So, he made him to understand with the words of a child that it is unlawful. Similarly, if a person calls a bird or beast with particular words, it responds to him and it does not respond to any other words. So be not indifferent to these words.

Classes of Repentants

The repentants are of four classes.

1. The First Class of Repentants:

1. The first class are those who repent for sins that may be committed up to the end of their lives and those who repent for past sins and take care not to commit sins in the future. As a result of habits, some evil thoughts may arise in his mind. For this, one should stay on repentance, advance towards good deeds, and give up evil ones. The name of his Tauba is Tauba Nasuha, or sincere repentance. The mind of such a repentant is called Nafse Mutmainna or quiet mind. It returns to its Lord well pleased with him and well pleasing Him-89:26. The Prophet said with regard to these persons "Muffarredun went in advance." They are desirous of God's remembrance. Zikr has pulled down from them their burdens. So, they will come with light burdens on the Resurrection Day. It is seen that there is the burden of Zikr on them, but actually it is Zikr which has taken away their burden. They have different ranks. There are some repentants whose desires fall under the flow of divine knowledge and become quiet. Another class of repentants cannot save themselves from clash with their low desires and they take delay to turn them back with efforts. There are some persons who meet with death after repentance. Some persons make Jihad with their passion after Tauba, keep patience and remain upon Tauba. Their rank is highest as their good deeds destroy their evil deeds. A certain sage said: If a sinner commits a sin and restraints himself from it after getting opportunity of committing it again out of fear

of God and keeps patience and controls his sexual desire, it expiates his sins. This condition is very difficult, but its result is very good.

2. The second class of repentants.

Such a person after repentance keeps himself firm for some days, gives up major sins and does divine service, but he is not free from such sins owing to pressure of circumstance although he has got no such object. He does not have a firm will to do that sin but if he commits it, he becomes repentant and sorrowful. Then he resolves that he will not do it again. The mind which has got such a state is called Nafse Lawwamah or self-accusing soul. This Tauba is less than that of the first class. Evil is mixed with the blood of man, and he can hardly release himself from it. God says: God is open handed in pardoning those who give up major sins and indecencies except passing thoughts of sins. An evil thought suddenly crops up in mind along with the minor sins. He had no previous thought about it. So, this kind of evil thought is pardonable. God says: When they do indecent acts or oppress themselves and then remember God and seek forgiveness for their sins. So, it is seen that God praised them for their repentance in spite of oppression on their soul. For this rank, the Prophet said: Those who repent after commission of a sin are the best among you. In another narration, a believer is like a stalk of corn. Sometime its head rises up straight and sometimes bends down. The Prophet said: A believer is not free from sin.

This shows that Tauba is not called for these sins. Such a guilty person does not reach the stage of a sinner. The Prophet said: Every son of Adam is a sinner. Among the sinners. those persons are good who repent and seek forgiveness. He said also a believer may commit many sins but is busy in repentance. God says: "They will be given double rewards on account of their patience and thereby remove the evils by good deeds." God says in this verse that they do good deeds after commission of a sin. He did not say that they do not commit sins.

3. The third class of repentants:
Such a repentant keeps himself all right for some time, and then his passion becomes strong for commission of sins. As a result, he advances towards sin, being unable to control his passion. In spite of this he does divine service always but cannot give up one or two sinful actions. He loves that it would have been better if God gave him power to control them. After the sin, he becomes repentant and says: "Alas, had I not done it." This soul is called Nafse Mosawaalah or questioning soul. God says regarding these persons "And about others, they recognize their sins, and they mix good works with them, and other mix evil deeds." These persons continue to do good deeds and expect forgiveness for their sins and faults. Many a time such a man dies before repentance. The reign of the next world and its enjoyment falls on that person whose soul is saved and who purifies his soul for a long time as decreed by God in his destiny. For this reason, God says: By the oath of soul and what it purifies, He informs of its evil deeds and its God-fear. He gets salvation, who purifies it, and he is ruined who pollutes it-91: 7. The Prophet said: A man may continue to do good deeds up to seventy years. Even the people then say that he is one of the inmates of Paradise. There is then the distance of half a cubit between him and Paradise. Then suddenly his fate comes forward and he begins to work the deeds of the inmates of Hell and then he enters Hell. So, there is the fear of death before his Tauba. Man's every breath may be his last breath and death may be linked up with that breath.

4. **Fourth class of repentants:**

These persons repent and remain in that condition for some days and then again return to sin. They feel no sorrow for their sins and do not mind to repent. These persons are included within the habitual sinners. Such a soul is called Nafse Ammarah or a soul prone the evils. Such a soul runs towards evils after returning from good deeds. There is fear for such a man in the end. If he dies upon evils, he will be an unfortunate person. If he dies upon good and upon Tauba, he will await his release from Hell although it will occur after some time. So, to seek forgiveness by divine service is like acquiring education by efforts and like seeking wealth by trade be crossing the big seas. All the people, except the learned are deprived of fortune. All the learned men except those who do good deeds are deprived of fortune. All the doers of good deeds are deprived of fortune except those who sincerely do good for the sake of God. They also remain in anxieties. Those who hope for God's forgiveness without any good deed at their credit are fools, as God says: "There is nothing for man except what he strives for." The wealth of the world is short-lived, still it is subject to hard labour. How can you expect rewards without hard labour and sincere efforts in the next world?

Expiation of Voluntary and Involuntary Sins

If a man commits a sin, he has got two compulsory duties-Tauba or repentance, and then doing good deed. A thing can be destroyed by its opposite, such as cold by heat. So, a bad deed can be removed by a good deed done immediately after it. If the evil deed rises from mind, its expiation is to seek forgiveness with all the humility of a slave. Expiation by tongue is admission of evil and seeking forgiveness from God saying, O Lord, I have done oppression to my soul and committed sin. So, forgive my sins. Expiation by bodily limb is to pray to give charity, and to do divine services.

It appears from the sayings of the sages that after the commission of a sin, if eight good deeds are done, it may be forgiven. The actions of heart regarding expiation of sins are four-Tauba, to think of good things, to take precautions of sin and to fear punishment for sins and for that to expect forgiveness. The actions of limbs are four regarding expiation of sins-(1) To pray two rak'ats immediately after commission of a sin, (2) then to pray for forgiveness to God seventy times and to recite (God is great with His praise) one hundred times, (3) to give charity, and then (4) to keep fast. Some wise man said: "After sin, make ablution well and pray two rak'ats in a mosque.' There is in a Hadis: When you commit a sin, do a god deed immediately, pray secretly if you do a sinful act secretly and pray openly if you do a sinful act openly. A certain sage said: "Sin committed at night is expiated by secret charity, and sin committed at daytime is expiated by open charity.

There is a Hadis: A man came to the Prophet and said I have committed every sort of sin with a woman except fornication. Give judgement against me according to the laws of God. The Prophet said: Have you not said this morning prayer with us? He said, "Yes, I have prayed." The Prophet said: "Certainly good deeds remove evil ones." It appears from this that except fornication, any other act with a strange woman is a minor sin. The minor sins committed during five prayers are expiated by these prayers.

Different stages of seeking forgiveness.

Hazrat Sahal Tastari said, "It is necessary for a slave to approach his master in every condition. So, it is better to return to the master in every matter. If he commits a sin says: O, Lord keeps it secret. When he finishes his sinful act, he says: O Lord accept my repentance. When he repents, he says: "O Lord make me sinless." When he does an act, he says: O Lord, accept this from me. Once a man asked him about such seeking of forgiveness expiation of sins. He said the beginning of seeking forgiveness is Izlijabat, then Inabat and then Tauba. Izlijabat means seeking forgiveness by moving bodily limbs. Inabat means mental act of seeking forgiveness by sincere motive and good wishes. Tauba means to give up the people and to return to the Creator. After Tauba he shall take recourse to silence and remain upon Tauba. The object of Tauba is to get two benefits-firstly, to expiate for sins in such a way that he can be classed with the man who did not commit sin: secondly, to gain such a rank as he can be addressed as a friend.

There are several steps for expiation of sins. Some steps efface the root of evil from its root. Some steps make the sin light. Expiation differs according to the rank of repentants. Don't think a good thing as insignificant even if it is very small. A certain foolish woman in order to ward off the troubles of weaving thread says. I can prepare only one piece of thread in an hour. What will you ll you do with one piece of thread? Can a piece of cloth be made with one piece of thread only? The foolish woman does not know that all the cloths in the world are woven with so many threads and the world in spite of its spaciousness, was created by so many atoms. In short to seek forgiveness and to express humility before God is such virtuous act which will never be destroyed.

A Certain disciple asked his Pir Abu Osman Maghribi, 'Sometimes my tongue utters Zikr and Quran-reading, but my mind remains then absent.' He said: "Be grateful to God that He kept one of your organs in a virtuous act, habituated you in Zikr, and has not engaged you in evil deeds." The saying of the sage is indeed true. If you can habituate your bodily limps in good works till it turns into habit, you will be removing great many sins. If a man has got the habit of uttering. "Astaghferullah" I seek forgiveness. of God, he will at once say "Astaghferullah" if he hears a false talk from anybody. For this reason, God says: "God does not spoil the records, of the doers of good." God says: "If you do a good deed, He will increase it and give you profuse rewards from Him." Hazrat Jafar Sadeq said, "God kept three things secret in three things -(1) His pleasure in divine services, so don't neglect anything of the divine service perhaps there lies His pleasure therein. (2) His wrath in sins. So do not neglect a trifling thing, as there may be His wrath therein. (5) His secret friendship amongst His servants. So don't disregard any of them, as he may be a friend of God. He added another thing-His hidden answer in his invocation. So don't give up invocation, often a reply may come therein.

Medicine for Unwillingness to Repent

There are two classes of men. One class of young men have got no attraction towards evil. They grow on good things and give up evils. The Prophet said: your Lord is pleased with that young man who has got no attraction towards evils, such a man is rare, but most honoured. The second class of men are not free from attraction towards evil. They are subdivided into two-those who repent after commission of sins and those who are engaged in sins all the time.

Tauba cannot be earned without curable medicine. He who cannot diagnose is a disease cannot know its medicine. Every disease has got its primary or root cause and to remove that cause is its medicine. Without an opposite thing, it can not be removed. Greed and negligence are the causes of engagement in sins. Carefulness is opposite to negligence and patience is opposite to greed. Negligence is the root of all evils. God says: They are negligent, there is no doubt that they will be losers in the next world. The medicine of Tauba is the mixture of some ingredients, sweetness of knowledge and bitterness of patience. A mind affected with the disease of repeatedly committing sins should be treated with a mixture of knowledge and patience.

Question: Is every knowledge profitable for removal of repeated sins?

Answer. There is expert knowledge about a special disease, just as the science of treatment is necessary for treatment of general diseases. A man of this type of disease must have faith in several objects.

I. He must have faith that there are certain causes of disease and health. God has recorded their causes and given us freedom to select those causes. Firm faith grows out of it in the root science of medicine as he who has no faith in this science will not take to treatment and has got nothing out ruin. Similarly, repeated commission of sin cannot be removed without faith in the fundamental matters of religion. That in this. There are causes of fortunes in the next world, and those causes are virtues, and there are causes of misfortunes in the next world, and those causes are sins. This is the faith in the basic principle of religion.

II. The second subject is that a patient must have faith in a certain physician that he has got expert knowledge in a particular branch of medicine an special proficiency in the process of treatment Similarly the sinner must have faith in the fact that the prophet is a true Prophet and all that he said are true without the slightest tinge of falsehood.

III. The third subject is that as a patient must obey with attention and care the instructions of the physician regarding diet and other injurious things, so also one addicted to sin must hear the verses of the Quran and the sayings of the Prophet with attention or follow these instructions with fear of God.

IV. The fourth subject is that as a patient must have look to what the physician gives instructions, so also every man should pay attention to what a spiritual guide says, though he has no greed for everything and does not commit every kind of sin. Every believer has got a special sin. The learned men of religion know about these and give instructions. accordingly. They must take the lessons of religion to the people according to their diseases. This world is the abode of patients or hospital, as there are only dead men under the earth and patients above the earth. The number of patients of heart disease is more than that of the patients of bodily diseases. The learned spiritual men are the physicians of heart diseases, and the kings are the caretakers of the hospitals. The patient which does not take the medicine of a learned man should be handed over to the king, so that he may cure him of this evil as a physician hand over a patient who does not observe the rules or who is mad.

Disease of the soul.

It is more severe than that of the body. There are three causes for which the disease of the soul is more severe than the disease of body. The first cause is that the patient does not know that he is sick. The second cause is that the result of the disease of soul is not seen in the world as the disease of body is seen. That death is the result of bodily disease is seen and one does not like it. Death of soul is the ultimate result of sin. That is not seen in the world and for this reason hatred for sin is less. If however the sinner knows it even you will see that he depends more upon God's mercy for cure of the disease of soul. He works very hard by giving up idleness for cure of the bodily disease, but he does not work so much for cure of the disease of soul. The third cause is that no physician can diagnose this incurable disease. The learned men are the physicians, and they are also attacked with the incurable diseases of the age and so they are baffled in their treatment. This disease is not openly seen as it exists in everybody. They teach such things to the people as increase their disease, as love of this world is their serious disease. This disease is found in the physicians themselves. They are said: You are talking about treatment but you yourselves have forgotten it. The people are going to destruction on account of the death of physicians as the physicians themselves are engaged in eating evil and injurious diets.

Hope and fear are two medicines, but they are applicable to various diseases. He whose fear is strong has given up this world wholly and burdened himself with additional burdens and confined himself within narrow provision. To him, the causes of hope are many while the causes of fear are few. He who repeatedly commits sins and is despaired of repentance for many sins in spite of his will for repentance should be treated with the cause of hope so that he may expect acceptance of his repentance. If he who is misguided and engaged in sins and still hopes for God's mercy, is like that person who is treated with honey in spite of his body being very heated. This is the way of the fools and the illiterate.

There are Four Modes of Giving up Sins

1.The first mode -

Is to remind the verses of fear to the sinner and transgressor. The Prophet said: The sun does not rise, and no darkness comes down without the two angels communicating with each other by four voices. One angel says: How good it would have been if after creation of men they knew the cause of their creation. Again, the first angel says: How good it would have been if after knowing the cause of creation of men they worked according to their knowledge. In another narration, how good it would have been if they discussed with one another about what they knew. Another angel says: How good it would have been if they repented for not doing what they knew. An earlier sage said: When a man commits a sin, the angel of the right side calls the angel of the left side: Don't write it for six hours with your pen. If he repents and seeks forgiveness, he does not write it. If he does not seek forgiveness, he writes it. Another ancient sage said When a man commits a sin, the ground underneath that place seeks permission to sink down with him under the abyss and the sky above his head seeks permission to fall upon him. Then God say to that ground and the sky: Keep yourself away from My servant and leave him, as you have not created him. If you had created him, you would have shown him mercy. Perchance he will repent to Me, and I may accept his repentance. Perchance he will do good works in place of it, and I will grant him reward. In the spirit of this, God says: God restrains the heavens and the earth to fall down. If they fall down, who is there besides Him to hold them back?

There is a tradition reported by Hazrat Omar: One who gives seal hangs down with the pillars of the Torone. When somebody tears of this hidden screen and considers an unlawful thing as lawful, God sends down a sealer to seal upon his soul. As a result, what is with it becomes covered. There is a tradition reported by Mujahed: Soul is like the front of an open hand. When a man commits a sin, a finger is closed down. When all the fingers are closed, the soul is closed. This is the meaning of seal. Hazrat Hasan Basari said: There is a fixed limit between man and his Creator. When he reaches that limit, God Himself puts a seal on his soul. Thereafter, he finds no inclination to do good deeds.

There are many traditions and wise sayings about punishment of sin and praise of those who repent. If one inherits from the Prophet, he should make much admonition there with. The Prophet left no legacy but left only learning and wisdom. The more he gets learning therefrom, the more legacy he gets from him.

2. Second mode:

To narrate the lives of the Prophets and of the saints and pious men and of the dangers and difficulties that fell on them on account of their sins are profitable for the souls of men and fruitful. It is also to be narrated how the Prophet Adam was punished for only one sin and how he was driven out of Paradise. It is narrated that when he ate the fruits of the forbidden tree, his dress flew away from his body and his private parts became exposed put his headgear and cover of his face felt shame to go away from him.

Then Gabriel came down and took his headgear and cover of his face. Then it was proclaimed from heaven: Go down from Me, as he who disobeys Me is not worthy to remain with Me. Hazrat Adam looked towards Hawa and saw that she was weeping. He said: This is the first sign of our disobedience to God.

It was narrated that for forty days an idol was worshipped in the house of the Prophet Solaiman for which he was punished. In another narration woman sought justice from Solaiman in respect of a matter of her father. He promised to do justice but afterwards he did not do it. In another narration, the woman thought that Hazrat Solaiman would deliver judgement in favour of her father as she had some rank before Solaiman. For this sin, the reign of Solaiman was robbed for forty days for which he became afraid. He fell into such disaster that he did not even get food when he was hungry. When he sought for food saying: Give me food, I am Solaiman, son of David, the people used to rebuke and beat him and drive him out. It was narrated that during this time when he wanted food from his wife she spat on his face and drove him out. There is another narration that an old woman poured urine over his head from a pot. Then God took out his ring from the stomach of a fish and he put it on for forty days after his punishment. Thereafter birds came and sat upon his head and jinn, birds and beasts began to gather around him. Solaiman said I will not rebuke you for harsh treatment with me before and will not praise you for your excuse before me at present. These affairs came from God and there was no other alternative.

There is a story of Banu Israil that a man married a foreign woman in her country. He sent his slave to bring her home. On the way the slave felt sexual desire to cohabit with her but restrained himself with great difficulties. For his patience, God rewarded him with the office of prophethood over the children of Israil. It was narrated that Moses once asked Khizr. Why has God given you knowledge of the unseen? He said: for giving up sins in order to incur the pleasure of God.

It is said that even wind travelled with Solaiman. He was once pleased with his dress and looked at it. Suddenly the wind threw him down, and he said: I obeyed you till you obeyed God. It is narrated that God sent down revelation to Hazrat Yakub: Do you know why I have separated your son Yusuf from you? He said: I don't know. God said: The reason is that you said to your sons When you remain indifferent, I fear lest tiger may devour him. Why did you fear for him an attack of tiger and did not depend on Me? Why did you look at their heedlessness and did not hope for my protection? Do you know why I returned him to you? Hazrat Yaqub said: I don't know, He said: You relied on Me and said: Perchance God may return all of them to me. You said also: Go and search for Yusuf and his brother and be not despaired. When Hazrat Yusuf said to his prisoner: Remind me to your master, God said: The devil made him forgetful of his Lord. For that, he stayed in prison for some years.

Thus, there are many stories. The Quran and Hadis did not narrate them only for the sake of stories, but its object is to admonish and to disclose the secret meaning, so that you may know that even Prophets were not free from these sins. So how can the other people get free from major sins? The Prophets received punishment in this world for minor sins and it was not kept in abeyance for the next world. The unfortunate only are given time, so that their sins may increase; as the punishment of the hereafter is very severe and most fearful. These stories should be narrated to the sinners; so that they may adopt the modes of repentance.

3. Third mode:
The sinners should be told that the punishment of sins is expected to be meted out in this world and that the basic cause of dangers and difficulties that befall on men is their sins. May people think the next worldly punishment as easy and this worldly punishment as severe. The reason is their ignorance about the next world. These people should be told repeatedly about the punishment of this world. They should be told that their livelihood may be curtailed on account of their sins, their honour may be marred, and their enemies may increase. The Prophet said: When a man commits sins, he is deprived of his livelihood. Hazrat Ibn Musud said: I think that a man forgets his learning owing to his commission of sins. In this context the Prophet said: Wisdom goes away from a man who commits sins, and it never comes to him. An ancient sage said: It is not misfortune that a man's face become black, and he meets with loss of property, but misfortune is that he gives up a sin but commits it again or a more heinous sin.

There is a story of a certain Aref that he was walking in a muddy land raising up his wearing apparel for fear of slipping down. Then he slipped and he fell down. He wept and said: My slip has been like the slip of one who walks by the side of a sin for saving himself from the sin and then slips into a sin or two and then falls deeply therein. For this reason, the saint Fazil said: Whatever turn of fortune and loss of friendship occur, it is only for your sin. A certain sage said. I will consider the oppression of rats as punishment of my sin. A certain Sufi of Syria said: I was looking at the beautiful face of a Christian boy. At that time Ibn Jala Dameski was passing by that way. He caught hold of my hand and I was ashamed. I said, O Abu Abdullah, glory to God. I was charmed with the uncommon beauty of this boy. I don't know the wisdom of God that he created this beautiful boy for Hell. He pressed my hand and said: You will see its punishment after a while. After 10 years I saw its punishment.

Abu Sulaiman Darani said: Emission of semen in dream is a punishment He said: Nobody misses a congregational prayer except for sins. There is in Hadis, God says: When a man puts his greed above his divine service, the lowest punishment is that I deprive him of the pleasure of invocation.

Abu Amer Osman narrated a story to this effect: I stood up for prayer when I felt urge of sexual passion which continued long. I felt a strong urge for cohabitation with a boy. I fell down on the ground and my whole body became black. Then I concealed myself and did not come out for three days. I went to the public bathroom and washed my body but it increased blackness. After three days, the blood of the body became clean. Then I went to Bagdad to meet Hazrat Junaid. I asked him about it. He said: Are you not ashamed that you have made your sexual passion strong after standing before God? Then God drove you out from His presence. Had I not prayed for you and repented on your behalf to God you would have met with that colour. He said: I wondered how he came to know of it, when I was at Rekka, and he was in Bagdad.

Dear readers, know that the face of soul of a man becomes black if he commits sins. If he is not a virtuous man, his black colour spreads over his face. If he is unfortunate, it remains on his soul which becomes black and becomes fit to be burnt by fire. The disaster of sin in the world is poverty, illness, and other evils as seen in various traditions. If any disaster comes to any person, it is owing to his sin. He is deprived of good provision, and his misfortune is doubled. If any grace reaches him, it is prolonged for him, but he is deprived of expressing gratefulness, till he is punished for ungratefulness. He who is virtuous, has blessing for divine service. He is then given grace of expressing gratefulness and his disaster is a panacea for his sins and increases his rank.

4. Fourth Mode:

It is to state the prescribed sentences for the prescribed crimes, such as drinking wine, fornication, murder, slander, and other sins. Give such advice to a person for which he is deserving of advice. If you give such advice to a person for which he is not deserving, you will be giving medicine to a person who does not require it. The learned man should begin treatment just like an experienced physician who sees first his patient's appearance. The Prophet was once asked: 0 Messenger of God, give me advice but not more. He said: Don't be angry. Another person said: O messenger of God, give me advice. The Prophet said: Don't be disappointed at seeing what is in the possession of man. This is called freedom from want. Be careful of greed, as the meaning of greed is freedom from the worldly wants. Pray in such a manner that you are leaving the world for good. Be careful of what you take as an excuse.

A person said to Ibn Wase: Give me advice. He said, I advise you to be angel in this world and the world next. He said: How shall I be able to become such? He said: Adopt renunciation in the world. The Prophet sensed anger in the mind of the first questioner. So, he prohibited him to get angry. He saw in the second greed man for wealth and i long hope and advised him accordingly. Hon Wase saw in the third person attachment towards the world and so he advised him accordingly. A man asked Hazrat Ma'az: Give advice. He said: Be kind, I may then guarantee Paradise for you. He perceived in him by his foresight harsh conduct and hard heart. Once a man said to

Ibrahim Ibn Adham: Give me advice. He said: Be careful of men and keep company of the virtuous people, as men are subjects of thoughts of men. Every man is not a real man. Real men passed away and there remain only ghosts. I don't consider them as man.

Hazrat Muawyiah wrote a letter to Hazrat Ayesha: Give me advice but no more. Hazrat Ayesha wrote: From Ayesh to Muawiyah, I heard from the Prophet who said: 'God makes one free from want of men who seeks pleasure of God by incurring the displeasure of men and He entrusts one to the people who incurs displeasure of God by pleasing the people, Salam to you' Now look to the wisdom of Hazrat Ayesha, how she gave caution of danger of the rulers. At another time she wrote to Muawiyah: Fear God, He will protect you from men and when you will fear men, they will not be able to do you benefit in presence of God, Salam to you." So, every adviser should advise according to the necessity of a particular man.

There are foods and medicines in theological learnings, food for all people and medicine for patients only. An illustration is given below. A man said to Abu Sayeed Khodri: Give me advice. He said: Fear God as it is the root of all good. Take recourse to Jihad, as there is no monkery in Islam. Take to the Quran, as it is the light for you among the inhabitants of the world and as it is a reminder to the inhabitants of heaven. Take to silence as you will drive away the devil therewith.

Once a man said to Hasan Basari: Give me advice. He said: Honour the commandments of God, God will honour you. The wise Loqman advised his son: O my darling, attach your lance with the learned, but dispute not with them, lest they may cherish hatred for you. Take from the world what is absolutely necessary for you and spend for your next world your excess wealth. Don't put your own burden to the shoulder of others by giving up completely this world. Keep fast in such a way as can destroy your greed and fast not in such a way as may spoil your prayer as prayer is better than fasting. Don't mix with the fools and hypocrites. He said to his son another time: O my darling, don't do any work with displeasure, Don't go out on a journey without necessity. Don't ask a thing which will not be beneficial to you. Don't squander your wealth and don't consider the wealth of others as good. What you send in advance is your wealth and what you leave behind is the wealth of others. O my darling, he who is kind gets kindness. He who keeps silent remains secure. He who speaks good gets benefit and he who speaks evil, commits sin. He who does not control his tongue becomes repentant. A man asked Hazrat Abu Hazem: Give me advice. He said: Do what will benefit you at the time of death and give up what will go against you at the time of death.

Hazrat Moses said to Khizr; Give me advice. He said: Walk with a smiling face and don't walk with an angry face. Be a benefactor and not an injurious man. Give up disputation and walk not without necessity, don't laugh out without being satisfied and don't accuse the sinners without sharing in their sins, O son of Imran, weep for four faults.

A man said to Mohammad bin Keran: Give me advice. He said: Make efforts to please your Creator as you make efforts to satisfy yourself. A man asked Hamid Lefafa: Give me advice. He said: See that disasters and dangers may not destroy your religion. Prepare for it a cover like that of the Quran. He asked: What is the cover of religion? He said: To give up search of this world except for things absolutely necessary, not to talk except what is absolutely necessary and to give up the company of men except for dire necessity.

Hazrat Hasan Basari wrote to Caliph Abdul Aziz: After praise of God and blessings on the Prophet-fear what God said to be feared. Be careful of what God said to be careful. Take for your fortune from what is in your possession. Sure, news will come to you at the time of your death, Salam to you.

Caliph Omar-b-Abdul Aziz wrote to Hazrat Hasan Basri Write to me a letter advising me. He wrote in reply: After praise of God and blessing on His Prophet, cares and disasters lie before you. Either you must meet with salvation or with destruction. Know that one who takes account of himself gets benefit and he who is unmindful is a loser. He who sees the ultimate end gets salvation. He who conducts himself with greed is misguided. He who keeps patience rises above wants. He who fears God is secure. He who is secure, accepts advice. He who accepts advice is blessed with deep insight. He who is blessed with deep insight gets understanding and wisdom. He who slips returns. He who repents uproots evils. Ask when you know not, and restrain anger.

The saint Maruf wrote to Caliph Omar-b-Abdul Aziz: After praise of God and blessing on His Prophet, O commander of the faithful, this world is an abode of punishment. He who has got no wisdom hoards wealth for it. He who has got no wisdom is deceived thereby. Live in this world as one who treats his wound and keeps patience at the bitterness of medicines fearing the result of disease. Caliph Omar- b-Abdul Aziz wrote to Adi-b-Artata: After Hamd and Salat, this world is an enemy of God's friends and a friend of the foes of God. It is an object of reception for the foes of God. He wrote to one of his governors: After praise of God and blessing on His Prophet, your power has been usurped from the oppression of the people. When you intend to do oppression on anyone, remember

God's power on you. Know that what reaches from you to the people will pass away, but it will remain with you. Know that God will obtain for the oppressed people the rewards of the oppressors. Salam to you.

Such are the forms of admonition and advise to the people. Such sort of advice is like from which everyone gets benefit. Such advisers are rare as the doors of advice have been closed and sin and disturbance gained ground. This is the first mode of treatment and the first root.

The second root is patience:

The basic medicine of repeated sins is patience. Why is patience necessary? One reason is that the sinner is careless about the injurious effect of good. Another reason is that his greed becomes strong. We have described the medicine for carelessness. Now we shall narrate the medicine of greed. The gist of it is that when a patient's injuries increase, his mode of treatment is that first of all he must have knowledge of the injury and then remove it so that it may not come to him again. In every circumstance, the bitterness of patience shall have to be adopted. There should be similar treatment of sexual passion. He should first know the injurious effect of sin and think of the verses of the Quran and Hadis about it. When fear increased, he shall have to remove the cause which increase the sexual passion. It grows out of outward things. To flee away from those things and to adopt loneliness are the medicines. The medicine of the greed of delicious foods is to remain hungry and to fast consecutive days. Without patience, these two modes cannot be adopted. Without knowledge, fear does not grow. Knowledge also cannot arise without insight, thoughts, and strong blind faith. The first thing is to be present in the assembly of Zikr and sermons and then to hear religious sermons after giving up all thoughts of the world. God makes the path of one easy who has been given the strength of good attention, who fears God after knowing the objects of fear, who hopes for rewards and knows good words as true; and He makes the path of one difficult who straightens his hands, thinks himself above wants and knows the true things as false.

Causes of Commission of Sins

1.First cause:

The punishment of sin is not presently seen and lies in the womb of future.

2. Second cause:

It is the present taste of the greed which leads to the sinful act. His habit assumes strong from owing to love for sin. Habit is the fifth nature. The present taste over nature predominates over the future tastes. For this reason, God says, Never, rather you love the present and discards the future. God says: Rather you love the pleasure of the world's life. The gravity of this affair is rendered clear from this word of the Prophet: Paradise is surrounded by unpleasant things and Hell by greed. The Prophet said: God said to Gabriel after creation of Hell: Go and look at Hell. He saw it and said: By Thy glory, nobody will enter it if he hears of it. Then God surrounded it with things of greed and said to him: Go and look at it. Gabriel saw it and said: By Thy glory, I fear that there will be nobody who will not enter it. He created Paradise and said to Gabriel: Go and look at it. Gabriel saw it and said: By Thy glory, he who hears of it will want to enter it. Then He surrounded it with unpleasant things and said, go now and see it. He saw it and said: By Thy glory, I fear that nobody will enter it. Greed is connected with the present and punishment with the future. There are two reasons for the commission of a sin though the basic faith remains all right. He who becomes impatient of thirst and drinks icy water during illness does not deny the basic science of medicine and also does not deny that it is injurious to his health, but the greed of his thirst becomes then strong, and he becomes unable to face the difficulty of patience.

3. Third cause:

There is no such a sinner who does not wish to expiate his sins by repentance anu good works, but he makes delay to make repentance and expiation owing to the prevalence of long hope in him.

4. Fourth cause:

There is no such believer who does not cherish hope for forgiveness of his sins. He awaits for pardon relying on the mercy of God after committing sins. For these four causes a believer is engaged in committing sins over and again even though his basic faith remains all right. It is true that for the fifth reason, defect enters into his basic faith.

5. Fifth cause:

To entertain doubt about the Prophethood of Muhammad (P.H.). This is infidelity. Medicines for these five reasons shall have to be looked into. Such a man is like the patient whom the physician prohibits to eat injurious foods. If the patient entertains doubt about the expert physician, he does not pay attention to his advice. This is disbelief or infidelity.

Question: What are the medicines for those five causes?

Answer:

(1) The medicine for the first cause is to think of the delay of punishment in this way. What will occur in the future must happen. The future is near the thoughtful men, but death is nearer to a man than the lace of his shoes. What will inform him that the Hour is near? Then the affairs of the future happiness will become the matters of the present. Great efforts are undertaken to ward off future dangers in the world. For earning profits in business, merchants embark on deep seas and oceans and bear all sorts of hardships in journey. If one falls ill and if a physician informs him that if he drinks cold water, it will injure him and may lead him to death, he shall give it up at once for fear of death, even though cold water is agreeable to him and even though the pangs of death is short-lived. He does not fear, however, what will occur after death. He shall have to leave the word, and there is no escape from it. This world's life is temporary, not everlasting. Now it is an object of thought that he gives up an agreeable thing of this world relying on the word of a Christian physician, while he cannot give up the temporary pleasure of the world in expectation of future happiness relying on the words of the Prophet supported by miracles. The punishment of Hell is very much greater than of disease.

(2) The medicine for the second cause is that he shall give up the taste which is strong with efforts and say: IfI cannot give up this temporary happiness of this world's life, how can I get the everlasting happiness of the next world? When I can't bear the pangs of patience, how shall I bear the punishment of fire in Hell?

(3) Disease of delay in repentance may be removed in this way. Most of the inmates of Hell will shriek for long sufferings in

Hell. He who makes delay in repentances, wishes to live long while he may die soon. If he lives long, he may not give up sin in future as he cannot give it up at present. It is not known how he will give up greed in future when he cannot give it up at present. Rather it may increase manifold owing to habits. The greed which man makes firm as a result of habits is not like that greed which has not become firmly rooted. For this reason, those who make delay in repentance are destroyed. They don't know that the more the time passes, the more it becomes difficult to be eradicated. The man of procrastination is like a man who seeing a firmly rooted tree, leaves it to be uprooted in future. But he knows that it will be more firmly rooted in future. The more you grow old, the more you will become weak and there will be less chance of your uprooting the tree.

(4) Medicine of waiting for God's forgiveness. He is like a person who spends all his wealth and makes himself and his family members poor in expectation of His mercy. He hopes that God will bring out a hidden treasure for him. out of uncultivated land. His waiting for seeking God's forgiveness for his sins is likewise.

(5) Medicine for the fifth cause. To doubt the prophethood of the Prophet in infidelity. Its medicine is the proofs of his being a true Prophet. He must be said: Is the affair in the next world impossible as the staying of a man in two different places at the same time is impossible? If he says: I have doubt in the next worldly affairs, he must be told: Eat the food which you have just left and into which someone has thrown poison. He shall not eat it believing a stranger's words. If he is a liar, you will still not eat the food, saying: I shall not eat it as it is

better for me to remain on the good side and to have patience. But if he is true, I shall meet with death if I eat it. So, to have patience is better than the pangs of death. Hazrat said to a man who had no faith in the next world: If what you say is true, we will get salvation. If it does not come out true, we shall get salvation, but you will perish. In other words, the wise man adopts always the path of safety. Such a disbeliever should be told: You give up food believing a stranger. How can you neglect the saying of the prophets, saints and wise men backed by miracles? There is no good in arguing with the illiterate. If there is difference of opinion among the wise regarding the next world, the deniers will suffer endless sufferings if it is true. If it is false, then only your temporary pleasures will suffer for some time. If anybody is wise, he must not doubt in this argument as there can be no comparison of these few days in this world with the everlasting nature of the next world. How can a wise man be able to earn everlasting happiness of the next world as he is engaged in the pleasure of the world?

The End.

www.ingramcontent.com/pod-product-compliance
Lightning Source LLC
Chambersburg PA
CBHW062144160726
48282CB00027B/943
* 9 7 8 9 3 9 4 7 7 0 5 6 0 *